Wired!

by Conn McQuinn

Welcome to the Lab! This book is guaranteed to amp up your interest in electronics!

Wired!

Published by SmartLab®, an imprint of becker&mayer!
All rights reserved. SmartLab® is a registered trademark of becker&mayer!, 11010 Northup Way, Bellevue, Washington.
Creative development by Jim Becker and Anna Johnson

If you have questions or comments about this product, send e-mail to info@smartlabtoys.com or visit www.smartlabtoys.com.

Edited by Betsy Henry Pringle
Written by Conn McQuinn
Art direction and packaging design by Scott Westgard
Book design, interior art direction, and illustrations by Eddee Helms
Assembly illustrations by John Laidlaw and Eddee Helms
Product photography by Keith Megay
SmartLab® character photography by Craig Harrold
Circuit design by Hunter Fulghum
Product development by Lillis Taylor
Production management by Katie Stephens
Project management by Beth Lenz

Printed, manufactured, and assembled in China.

Wired! is part of the SmartLab® *Electronics Lab* kit. Not to be sold separately.

10 9 8 7 6 5 4 3
0-9748486-3-8
05251

LET'S GET WIRED!

The parts in this kit allow you to explore the basic concepts of electricity. You will build burglar alarms, timers, and other amazing things that will make you look like an electronic genius!

Each project is a different *circuit*. A circuit is a term that means "a bunch of electronic components that does something when you send electricity through it." This one workbench setup will let you build twenty different circuits!

Before you do these projects, however, you need to prepare your workbench. First, you will install all of the little electronic parts in the plastic tray onto the top of the cardboard box with the holes punched in it. Once all these electronic parts, called *components*, are installed, then you will make your projects by hooking the components together with pieces of wire.

WHAT'S

Of course, **none** of these projects will do a thing without electricity.

SO JUST WHAT IS ELECTRICITY?

Everything you see around you—and a lot of stuff you can't see, like air—is made up of tiny particles called *atoms*. Atoms have even smaller parts called *electrons*. Under the right conditions and with the right materials, electrons can be made to jump from one atom to another. This movement of electrons from one atom to another is *electricity*. When you have a bunch of electrons moving in the same direction, it's called electricity or an *electrical current*.

As the word current might tell you, people often compare electricity to water. It "flows" through certain kinds of materials, called conductors. But instead of using plumbing, you build *circuits*.

Most of the components in your kit are things that change the flow of electricity. Some reduce it, some work like one-way valves, some work like faucet controls, and so on. The wires act like pipes to connect them together.

ELECTRICITY?

For all your circuits, the electricity will come from a battery acting as an electricity pump. A battery has a lot of extra electrons in one side, and not enough on the other side. When you connect the battery terminals (the metal parts on top), the electrons flow from the negative terminal (too many electrons), through the wire circuit, to the positive terminal (not enough electrons).

Electricty flows through metals. That's why we use wires to build the circuits. Metals that conduct electricity are called *conductors*.

Plastic, rubber, and glass are poor conductors. They are called *insulators*. The plastic insulator on the wires keeps the electricity from touching YOU!

① Do not use any other source of electricity with your projects. The current from wall sockets or appliances is very, very strong and can cause you great injury. There is no risk from the current in your battery, but anything more powerful will, at the very least, damage the circuits in your workbench. Or it could damage your circuits. Treat electricity with extreme care.

② Do not connect the two terminals of the battery directly together with a piece of wire or other material. The battery and wire will heat up enough to burn you!

PUTTING TOGETHER THE
SMART LAB

INSTALLING THE SPRINGS

The cardboard workbench with all the holes punched in it will form the base to the many cool circuits that you will build. The first step in transforming the box into your workbench is installing the springs that you will find in the plastic tray.

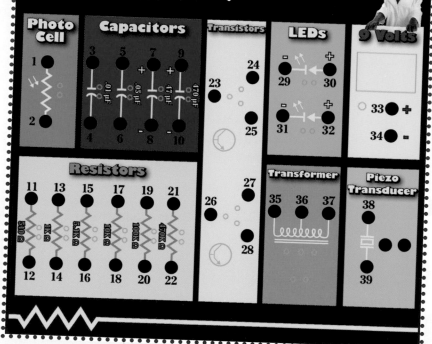

Push a spring, small end first, about halfway into each of the 39 bigger holes (they have a number next to them). After you have filled all the holes with springs, open the bottom of the box.

WORKBENCH

INSTALLING THE COMPONENTS

Component

Leads

Top of
Workbench

24

23

Holes

Springs

25

You are now ready to begin installing your components, but first these **WORDS OF WARNING:** Many of these parts will not work if they are not put in the right way, and some will get permanently zapped if they are put in wrong. Pay close attention to the directions or you'll be trotting down to your local electronic supply store for replacement parts!

TOP OF THE WORKBENCH

Look at the top of your workbench. Next to the springs are small holes.

Look at the components. Each component has two or three wires or *leads* coming off it. You are going to poke the leads through these small holes on the top of the workbench (the instructions will tell you which lead goes into which hole).

UNDERNEATH THE TOP

Underneath the top, you are going to insert each lead between the coils of the spring near it. You will do this by bending the spring with your finger and pushing the end of the lead into the coil.

Component
Wires

Underneath
Workbench

THE CAPACITORS

The first parts that you are going to install are called *capacitors*. You have four different capacitors for your workbench. Two of them look like little tan-colored disks. These are called ceramic capacitors. If you look closely, you will see that there is printing on the side. Find the smallest one—it should say "103" or ".01" on it. This is going to be the first component that you install.

Capacitors come in thousands of sizes and kinds, and are used mainly to provide a place in a circuit where the power of the electricity can build to a higher level.

FOLLOW THESE STEPS

1 **Poke the leads** from the bottom of the capacitor that says "103" or ".01" on it through the small holes on the top of the workbench next to springs 3 and 4. It doesn't make any difference which lead goes in which hole.

2 **Turn the box** over and bend spring 3 until you can insert the closest lead into one of the gaps. Once you have the wire lead in spring 3, let go of the spring.

3 **Insert the other** lead between the coils of spring 4.

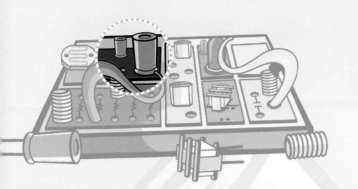

4 Put the capacitor numbered "503" or ".05" into holes and springs 5 and 6.

The other two capacitors look like small cans with two leads on the bottom. These are *electrolytic* (e-lek-tre-LIT-ik) capacitors. They store more electricity than ceramic capacitors. Another important difference is that these capacitors don't work if you put them in backward!

5 Find the capacitor that says "47μF" on the side. Look carefully, and you should be able to find one side that has a minus (-) sign on it. Put the lead under the minus sign through the small hole next to spring 8. Put the other lead through the hole next to spring 7. Attach them to the springs underneath. Now, double-check and make sure that the minus side of the capacitor is next to spring 8.

6 Now take the last capacitor (which should say "470μF" on the side) and put it into holes 9 and 10. Attach the lead from the minus side to spring 10.

THE RESISTORS

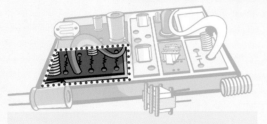

Resistors are components that reduce the flow of electricity. Even in materials that conduct electricity, there is always some resistance to the electricity.

Resistors are made to have a very specific level of resistance. They can be used to control how much electricity is traveling in a circuit, which is very important. Some of the components you have in your workbench need only small amounts of electricity. The battery produces more electricity than they need, and without resistors they would burn out. The electricity straight from the battery would make some circuits run too fast to be usable, so the resistors reduce the flow to a useful level.

If you look closely, you'll see that each resistor has colored stripes. The stripes indicate how strong the resistor is, and each color indicates a different number (except for a gold or silver one on the end). The stripes are pretty small, so you should try to work with a good light and look closely so you can tell the difference between a brown stripe and a purple stripe.

Resistance is like friction—it makes it hard to move the electricity through.

You should have six resistors.
They should be installed as follows:

1 Find the resistor with green, brown, and brown stripes. (The last brown stripe should be closest to the gold or silver stripe.) Install it in springs 11 and 12. It doesn't matter which way you put it in.

2 Install the resistor with brown, black, and red stripes in springs 13 and 14.

3 Install the resistor with green, brown, and red stripes in springs 15 and 16.

4 Install the resistor with brown, black, and orange stripes in springs 17 and 18.

5 Install the resistor with brown, black, and yellow stripes in springs 19 and 20.

6 Install the resistor with yellow, purple, and yellow stripes in springs 21 and 22.

THE PHOTOCELL

A photocell is a special kind of resistor—its resistance depends on how much light is shining on it. The darker it gets, the less electricity it lets through.

The photocell is the tiny disk with orange squiggles on the top. Attach it to springs 1 and 2. It doesn't matter which way you put it in.

THE TRANSISTORS

The two small black components with three leads sticking out the bottom are *transistors*. There are only two in your workbench, but they are very important. They are also very easy to break, so be careful!

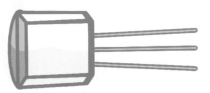

Transistors work like small electricity faucets. Electricity comes in the top leg and goes out the bottom leg. The middle leg turns the flow on and off. If even a little electricity comes into the middle leg, it will open the transistor and let a lot of electricity flow from the top leg to the bottom leg. If the middle leg doesn't get any electricity, then no electricity goes through.

A small amount of electricity here...

...results in a large amount of electricity here.

INSTALLING YOUR TRANSISTORS

Transistors play a huge part in most modern electronics. Here is how to install yours:

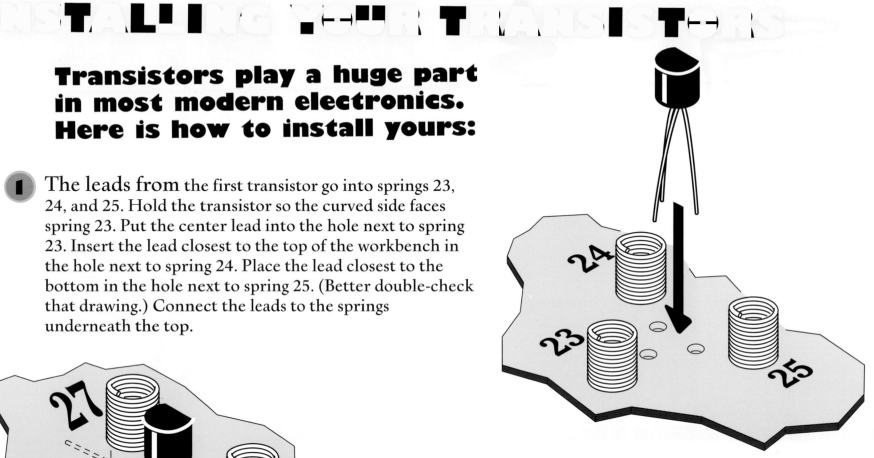

1 The leads from the first transistor go into springs 23, 24, and 25. Hold the transistor so the curved side faces spring 23. Put the center lead into the hole next to spring 23. Insert the lead closest to the top of the workbench in the hole next to spring 24. Place the lead closest to the bottom in the hole next to spring 25. (Better double-check that drawing.) Connect the leads to the springs underneath the top.

2 Install the leads from the second transistor in springs 26, 27, and 28. Face the curved side toward spring 26, and put the center lead into hole 26. Put the top lead into hole 27, and the bottom lead into hole 28. Connect the leads to the springs underneath the top.

ALL THE OTHER

THE
LEDS

The bright red and green "lights" are called *light-emitting diodes*, or LEDs for short. LEDs allow electricity to go in only one direction. However, they also light up, which makes them way cool!

If you look closely at the LEDs, you will notice that one side of the little edge around the bottom is flat. Put the red LED into springs 29 and 30, with the flat edge next to spring 29. Put the green LED into springs 31 and 32, with the flat side toward 31. Double-check the LEDs—if they're in backward, they'll stop the electricity from flowing!

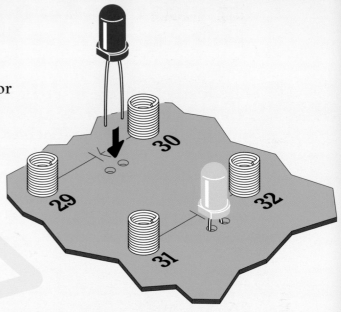

THE
TRANSFORMER

The large component with five leads coming out of it is called a *transformer*. A transformer is a device that transforms or changes the voltage of the electricity passing through it. Put it in the holes indicated in the drawing (the leads will match up exactly with the small holes) and attach the three long leads to springs 35, 36, 37.

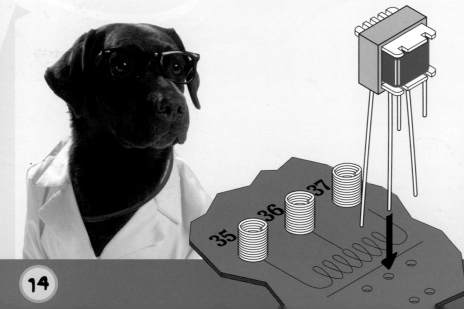

STUFF

THE PIEZO TRANSDUCER

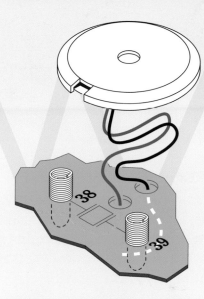

The big round disk is the *piezo transducer* (pronounced pea-AY-zoh, very Italian). It makes noise when electricity goes through it. Place the two leads on the piezo transducer through the two holes next to springs 38 and 39 as shown, then attach the leads to springs 38 and 39. Make sure the leads don't touch.

THE BATTERY

And last, but certainly not least, is the battery holder. Feed the red and black leads through the small hole next to spring 33. The red wire goes to spring 33, and the black wire to spring 34. (Definitely double-check this, because if you did this backward, nothing's going to work.) Place a 9-volt battery into the punched-out rectangle.

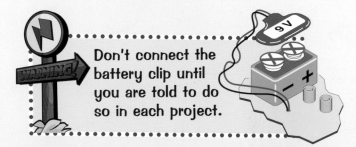

Don't connect the battery clip until you are told to do so in each project.

Whew! Congratulations! Your workbench is done!

Fold your workbench back together. You will have a bunch of hookup wires left over. Keep them in the plastic tray. You will use them for building your projects. However, there is one more step that we must take, and that is. . .

TESTING YOUR
SMART LAB

Before you get too far, it's a good idea to test your workbench and its components to make sure there are no problems. (It's a lot less frustrating to find problems and fix them now.) Here are a couple test circuits that, when hooked up, will make sure everything is doing what it is supposed to do.

> You will test your workbench by connecting wires to some of the springs on the top of the workbench. Connecting springs creates a circuit that connects the components.

SOME BASIC RULES
OF WIRING:

 Insert the metal end of each wire between the coils of the spring on the top of the workbench. Connect metal to metal. Make sure the wire (not the plastic wrap) is hooked in the spring.

 Gently pull the wires to make sure they are connected.

 Try not to bend the wires more than you have to. They will eventually break.

 Use the shortest wire possible. You might need the longer one somewhere else, and besides, it looks tidier.

 Last, but certainly very important: Never hook up the battery until you have the whole circuit completed. Hooking it up too early can fry your components.

WORKBENCH

TEST CIRCUIT #1: RED LED

Take your wires and hook up the following pairs of springs: 11 to 33, 12 to 30, 29 to 34. Attach the battery clip, and the red LED should light up. If it doesn't, make sure that the flat side of the LED is facing spring 29.

TEST CIRCUIT #2: GREEN LED

Hook up the following pairs of springs: 11 to 33, 12 to 32, and 31 to 34. Attach the battery clip, and the green LED should light up. If it doesn't, double-check that the flat side of the LED is facing spring 31.

TEST CIRCUIT #3: TRANSISTOR I

To test transistor 1 (springs 23, 24, and 25), connect the following pairs of springs: 11-33, 12-30, 17-23, 24-29, 25-34. Attach a long wire to spring 18, hook up the battery clip, and touch the other end of the long wire to spring 33. The red LED should light up. If it doesn't, then transistor 1 was not installed properly. Make sure the leads are in the right holes.

TEST CIRCUIT #1

TEST CIRCUIT #4: TRANSISTOR 2

To test the other transistor, connect the following pairs of springs: 11-33, 12-30, 17-26, 27-29, 28-34. Again, attach a wire to spring 18, hook up the battery clip, and then touch the other end of the wire to spring 33. If the red LED lights up, all systems are go! If not, double-check that all the leads are attached to the right springs.

GENERAL TROUBLESHOOTING

Sometimes you will find that a circuit won't work, even after you double-check all the connections. If this is the case, first check your battery by removing it and trying it in something else that uses a 9-volt battery. If the battery is okay, take all the wires off and start again from scratch, paying close attention to the directions. (This is frustrating, but it can be easier than tracking the problem down any other way.) If the circuit still doesn't work, you may have burned out a transistor. (They are fragile little guys.) Disconnect all the wires and try the transistor-checking circuits previously outlined.

If the transistor is not working, try your local electronic parts store and ask for a "general purpose NPN transistor, such as 2N2222 or 2N3904." No, they don't cost very much.

ANYTIME YOU ASSEMBLE THAT CIRCUIT, KEEP IN MIND THAT:

 Something is bound to go wrong eventually,

 You will become frustrated,

 This is perfectly normal and happens to **NASA** engineers, too,

 With a little patience and an I-can-do-it attitude, you should be able to find the problem and fix it.

These hints cover most of the problems you might encounter. The transistors and LEDs are the components voted "most likely to cause trouble," but the circuits on page 17 will allow easy testing of them. If they break, these components are available, inexpensively, at any electronic parts store.

If a circuit won't cooperate and you've done everything imaginable, then pack it in. Move on to another circuit, and come back to the problem circuit another day. There's a very good chance it will work perfectly.

EXPERIMENT 1
ENGINE SOUNDS

This circuit creates a realistic engine sound, just like an arcade game. Here are the hookups for this circuit:

7-35-38, 8-16-23, 15-33-36, 24-37-39, 25-34

Remember to connect the battery after you have made all the hookups!

WHAT'S GOING ON?

The noise you hear should sound like the revving engine of a car. That's because the circuit itself actually makes the sound the same way an engine does.

A car gets its power from a series of small rapid explosions inside the engine. Each explosion pushes hot gases out the tail-pipe—pop! When lots of these pops happen very quickly, the air in the pipe vibrates, and makes the familiar VROOM sound!

The next time you play with a handheld video game that makes a racing-car sound, you'll know that inside each of these is a circuit like this one.

So what's happening with the circuit? The circuit you built sends little zaps of electricity through the piezo transducer, and each time this happens the piezo transducer bends a tiny bit. After the electricity stops, the piezo transducer bends back to normal, which pushes a little puff of air out of the hole in the middle—pop!

SIREN WITH LIGHT

When you connect the battery, you will hear a tone. When you touch the loose end of the green wire to spring 18, the tone changes and the red LED lights up. Try touching and then removing the wire from the spring several times in a row to make a realistic siren sound.

This circuit makes a siren sound and also has a flashing LED. You will connect a green wire at one end and use the other end to touch another spring and create a siren sound. Here are the connections:

5-35, 6-15-20-23, 24-37-39, 11-19-33-36-38-GREEN WIRE, 25-28-34, 16-17, 18-21, 22-26, 12-30, 27-29

WHAT'S GOING ON?

The circuit incorporates something called an *oscillator* (no, it's not a cross between an ocelot and an alligator). An oscillator is a circuit that switches the electricity on and off very quickly—it switches from red to green and back again thousands of times every second. The electricity turns the piezo transducer on and off very quickly, making it vibrate. That's what makes the sound. Here, you control the oscillator by touching the wires together, which sends electricity to the oscillator and to the LED.

Sirens and flashing lights are, of course, very important for trying to get someone's attention.

That's why emergency vehicles use lights and sirens. The lights flash so rapidly and shine so brightly that they are almost impossible to ignore. They can be picked out of a background of lights from miles away. As for the sirens, they're more than just loud. The quick changing of the sound—EEEoooEEEooo—gets people's attention as well.

EXPERIMENT 3
LIGHT FADER

This circuit slowly turns off an LED. When you touch the loose end of the yellow wire to spring 19, the LED will shine brightly. When you remove the yellow wire from spring 19, the LED will slowly fade and then go off. These are the connections:

11-17-33, 12-30, 24-27-29, 25-26, 10-20-28-34, 18-YELLOW WIRE, 9-19-23

WHAT'S GOING ON?

This circuit uses a capacitor—a kind of storage tank that fills up with electricity instead of water. In this project, the capacitor fills up with electricity, and then passes it on to the part of the circuit where the LED is. The light slowly dims as the current flows out of the capacitor, and when the capacitor is finally empty, the light goes out.

Fading circuits are used in movie theaters to fade the lights slowly before the movie starts, which gives everyone a few minutes to get ready before the room gets totally dark. For instance, imagine there's a guy trying to squeeze past your legs as he struggles to balance four superlarge soft drinks, when the lights are suddenly turned off. You can imagine the advantages of a slow fade-out!

It's also nice to have the lights slowly fade on at the end of the movie. After you've been sitting in the dark for about two hours, it is not a pleasant experience to suddenly have a bunch of bright lights shining in your face.

Fading circuits are also used in video cameras (to get those spiffy fade-out and fade-in effects), stage lights, and the little lights inside cars.

22

TRAFFIC LIGHT

When you hook up the battery, the red and green LEDs will blink back and forth, just like a traffic light. The LEDs blink faster than usual, so you don't have to wait forever for the light to change as you would at a real stoplight. These are the connections:

9-29-24, 11-19-21-30-32, 8-20-23, 10-22-26, 7-27-31, 25-28-34, 12-33

WHAT'S GOING ON?

This circuit works like old-fashioned traffic lights, which had built-in timers that controlled when the lights changed color. These timers were mechanical devices using gears and switches to turn the lights on and off. The timer in your project is made from capacitors and resistors.

When the capacitor fills with enough electrical current, it changes which LED is lit. The size of the capacitor determines how long it will take to fill, which in turn controls how often the traffic light changes.

With timer-driven stoplights, you find yourself sitting at a red light, even when there's nobody else in sight. Nowadays, most traffic lights are "smart"—they have computers with pressure sensors that tell them when a car is waiting, so the light turns green as soon as the other street is clear.

Unfortunately, your stoplight is of the "dumb" variety, but that doesn't mean it can't be useful. Big lines at the bathroom in the morning? Put it by the sink to control how long people brush their teeth. Waiting for the pizza to get to you? Put the stoplight on the table and have the food rotate every time the light turns green.

BURGLAR ALARM

WHAT'S GOING ON?

This is one of the most common kinds of burglar alarm. Part of the circuit is a simple switch, with one part mounted on a door and the other on the doorframe. If the door is closed, the switch is connected and the current can go through. When the door is opened, the switch opens and the electricity can't get through, making the buzzer (actually the piezo transducer) sound off in its rather annoying style.

What a minute! If the switch is open and the electricity can't get through, shouldn't the piezo transducer be off? How can the piezo transducer work if the electricity isn't reaching it?

Good question! The circuit is set up so that the current can either pass through the switch or go through the piezo transducer. Either way makes a complete circuit. Electrical current is very practical, however (perhaps "lazy" would be a better term). It always takes the easier path it can find, and as it turns out, the part of the circuit with the piezo transducer has more resistance than the part with the switch. It's no contest—the current heads over the switch and ignores the piezo transducer.

However, when someone opens the door (and therefore the switch), the switch part of the circuit becomes a dead end. Suddenly the piezo transducer is the only game in town. The current heads on through, and the alarm buzzer goes on.

So there you have it. Now you can use the alarm in all sorts of ways. Hook it to your bedroom door to keep nosy brothers or sisters out (or to catch the tooth fairy in the act, assuming she uses the door). Wire the box containing your comic book collection to prevent unauthorized reading. Set up an alarm so that when your older brother tries to sneak into the house two hours past curfew everyone will know. (Unfortunately, while entertaining, this usually results in a squished circuit.)

MUSICAL ORGAN

This circuit uses pencil marks to make music! First, build the circuit following the connections below. Then find a piece of thin white paper and trace the funny shape below. Using a regular (not colored) pencil, color in the shape so it's really dark and there is no white showing through at all. Press one wire to the bottom of the pattern and the other to the end of one of the three lines. Make sure your finger doesn't touch the metal ends of the wire when you press the wire onto the pencil marks. Try each line for a different musical note! Here are the connections:

GREEN WIRE-17, GREEN WIRE-33-36-38, 4-18-19-23, 3-35, 24-37-39, 20-25-34

○ Trace this shape

WHAT'S GOING ON?

As you probably figured out already, there is an oscillator in this circuit.

But what about the pencil marks? Well, the "lead" in a pencil is mainly a material called graphite, which conducts electricity. When you put the wires at either end of the pencil line, electricity goes through the pencil line, making the oscillator oscillate and the piezo transducer speak.

However, graphite isn't a very good conductor. When the line you've drawn is really short, lots of electricity can get through. The longer the line is, the harder it is for the electricity to make it from one wire to the other—so less makes it to the circuit. That's why different lines make different sounds.

All electronic instruments use some variation of this circuit idea, whether they're keyboards or guitars. Who knows—maybe some day you'll be at a concert and the lead singer's keyboard will explode in a ball of sparks. He'll stand up and say, "Unless someone here can make me a new instrument, we'll have to cancel the concert." You'll grab your circuit, a sheet of paper and a pencil, race to the stage, and save the day!

All right, so that's a little much. But at least you have an idea of how the instruments work!

TOUCH-ACTIVATED SWITCH

This circuit turns on an LED when you simply touch a wire. To turn on the LED, hold the end of one yellow wire and, with your other hand, touch the end of the other one.
Here's how to hook this up:

YELLOW WIRE-11, YELLOW WIRE-13-17-33, 18-24, 12-23, 25-26, 14-30, 27-29, 28-34

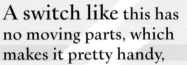

WHAT'S GOING ON?

Don't look now, but your body is part of this circuit!

Remember when we talked about conductors in the introduction? Well, our bodies are also conductors—after all, they're mostly water. As a matter of fact, we use electricity to run ourselves all the time. Your body uses electricity to control when the heart muscle pumps, when your lungs breathe in and out, and all the workings of all the other muscles and nerves in your body.

What's this got to do with your circuit? Touching the space between the wires turns you into part of the circuit. The current is going from one wire into your fingertip, through your skin, and into the other wire (don't worry, there isn't enough electricity in the circuit to hurt you). This works only because our bodies can conduct electricity.

A switch like this has no moving parts, which makes it pretty handy, since there is nothing to wear out or break. That's why you'll find lots of elevators with touch-activated switches, since they get pushed hundreds of times a day. These switches also work really well in places where regular switches would be too big, such as computer touch screens. These screens are covered with lots of tiny switches that turn on when you touch them, letting the computer know where your finger is.

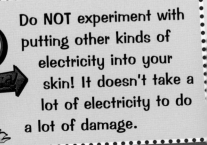

Do NOT experiment with putting other kinds of electricity into your skin! It doesn't take a lot of electricity to do a lot of damage.

SOUND-ACTIVATED SWITCH

This circuit uses sound waves to turn on the LED. After you connect the battery, clap right above the piezo and you'll see the LED light up. It will flash for an instant when the sound waves from your clap hit the piezo transducer. Try shouting really loudly and see if you can light up the LED. Here's how to hook it up:

11-17-21-33, 12-30, 24-29, 18-23-27, 19-22-26-38, 20-25-28-34-39

WHAT'S GOING ON?

The circuit you have built is designed to respond to a loud, sharp sound. When you clap your hands, it sends vibrations through the air. The vibrations make the disk inside the piezo transducer bend back and forth, which in turn makes a little bit of electricity. That little bit of electricity is just enough to start up the circuit and send enough electricity to the LEDs to light them up.

A device with a sound-activated switch can be used for lots of handy things. You've probably seen the ads on television for a little box you can plug your appliances into so you can turn them on and off with a clap of your hands. People who have a hard time moving around find this kind of assistance very helpful. Old-fashioned television remote controls worked on a similar principle, but used sounds so high-pitched that people couldn't hear them (although the neighborhood dogs probably hated them).

Of course, a sound-activated switch works best in a place that's normally pretty quiet. That's why they make good burglar alarms. Usually, a closed store or museum is a peaceful, quiet place. Any sudden or loud sounds are a good clue that someone is messing around inside, making a sound-sensitive alarm a good idea.

LIGHT-ACTIVATED SWITCH

This circuit uses light shining on the photocell to turn the LED on and off. Vary the amount of light on the photocell by going first into a dark room, such as a closet or bathroom. The LED should turn on. Then turn on the lights, and the LED should turn off. Experiment with different levels of light to see when the LED turns on and off by simply putting your hand over the photocell. Here are the connections:

19-24-33, 1-20-23, 25-30, 2-29-34

WHAT'S GOING ON?

The important part of this circuit is the photocell or *photoresistor*. The photoresistor controls the amount of electricity that can flow in response to light. In bright light the photoresistor has low resistance—electricity can easily go through it. In darkness, it has high resistance, and little or no electricity can squeeze by. Your circuit is designed to respond to the amount of electricity getting through the photocell. If the level of light reaching the photocell goes down too far, the LED goes on. When the room brightens again, the LED goes off.

Of course, the most common use for this idea is in porch lights, night-lights, and streetlights. In the old days (the "dark ages," you might say) somebody actually had to turn all the streetlights on and off. Now, each light has its own light-sensitive circuit so it can switch itself on and off.

If you have a night-light, there's a good chance it works the same way. See if it has a photocell and if it does, cover the photocell with your fingertip and see if you can trick the light into switching on. (The same trick works on streetlights, but it's a little harder to reach the photocell on a 25-foot-tall light pole.)

EXPERIMENT 10
LIGHT ORGAN

WHAT'S GOING ON?

This is an instrument that lets you play music with light. Once it's all hooked up, use this circuit in a well lit room. Wave your hands a few inches over the photocell to change the tone you hear. The less light there is on the photocell, the lower the tone. If you have trouble getting the tone to change, place an empty paper towel tube over the photocell (so only light from directly above will hit the photocell) and then move your hands over the tube. Here are the connections:

3-35-38, 4-20-21-26, 27-37-39, 1-33-36, 2-19, 22-28-34

You controlled sound in project #6 with pencil lines. This time, you'll use light. ("Lights! Circuit! Sound!")

The **current is** controlled by the light passing through the photocell. The electricity then goes into an oscillator. If there isn't much light, there isn't much electricity, and a low tone is produced. If there is a lot of light, there is a lot of electricity, and you get a high tone.

Photocells are used in lots of other ways, too. Cameras use them to keep pictures from getting too much or too little light. Photocells can help robots find their way around by helping them see where light and dark areas are in a room. Photocells have even been used in television sets to automatically adjust the brightness of the picture to match lighting in the room.

Dogs don't need circuits to make beautiful music. WOOF!

29

ELECTRONIC TIMER

WHAT'S GOING ON?

This is a capacitor-based circuit. When you connect the wires, electricity flows into the capacitor. When the capacitor is full, it has enough power to switch on the part of the circuit that lights up.

The capacitor works like a storage tank that holds water until you need it. Suppose you were mad at someone and you wanted to get even with them. What you really want to do is soak them—soak them good. The problem is that your water hose only trickles. What can you do? You can let the water trickle into a bucket. When it's full, you can use it to hit them with one big blast of water, instead of dribbling on them.

Capacitors work the same way. Even if you have a little flow of electricity, you can use a capacitor to store it up into a higher charge. The switch that turns on the light won't work until the capacitor has stored up enough electricity to make it go.

After the battery is hooked up, the timer will start when you touch the loose end of the yellow wire to spring 19. The red LED will light up and stay lit for 20 seconds and then turn off by itself (it's normal if the LED still looks like it's slightly lit even when it's off). Sometimes the timer will start itself when you connect the battery. If the LED is on when you connect the battery, wait about 20 seconds—it should turn off. These are the connections:

3-19, 4-16-17-24, 13-15-21-33-YELLOW WIRE, 18-26, 7-22-23, 8-27-29, 20-25-28-34, 14-30

You can also change the length of the timer by changing the capacitor. If you replace the 47uF capacitor with the 470uF capacitor you will change the timer from 20 seconds to about 2 minutes. Just take the wire in spring 8 and put it in 10, and also change 7 to 9.

The capacitor works like a timer. If you know how much electricity is going into the capacitor and how much charge it will hold, then you should be able to figure out how long it will take for it to fill up.

By making circuits that are just a tad more complicated than this one, it's possible to build extremely accurate clocks. Some sports depend on clocks that measure speed in thousandths of seconds. It's not possible for a stop watch to measure with such precision. Without electronic timers there would be lots more fighting over just how fast people are.

ELECTRONIC CANDLE

WHAT'S GOING ON?

After you hook up the circuit, blow hard into the piezo transducer. You should see the LED turn off. To turn the LED on, disconnect the battery and then reconnect it. Then you can blow it out again!
Here's what to hook up:

11-13-33, 14-15-27,
16-23, 17-26-38, 12-30,
18-24-29, 25-28-34-39

What won't they think of next! An electrical light you can blow out. All the excitement of a real candle—with none of the fiery risk! And all you need is a piezo transducer!

All right, you do need more than a piezo transducer, but it is the centerpiece of the project. When you blow into the piezo transducer, your breath bends the metal disk inside, producing a small electrical current. Even though it's an itty-bitty amount of electricity, it's enough to trigger the "off" switch in your circuit, and—zip—off goes your LED.

> So what's it good for? Believe it or not, there are practical applications of this idea.

One is weather. As the speed of the wind changes, the sound it makes blowing on a microphone changes. The microphone can be hooked up to a computer that will interpret the changes in sound and figure the speed of the wind.

You could measure, of all things, how much natural gas comes into your house. One type of meter has a small microphone that "listens" to how fast the gas is coming through it. A small computer attached to the microphone can use the speed information to figure out how much gas is being used.

EXPERIMENT 13
CONDUCTANCE CHECKER

WHAT'S GOING ON?

This circuit lets you test objects to see if they conduct electricity.

This is another circuit that has an oscillator and a piezo transducer. When you touch the wires to something that conducts, the electricity goes through and makes the sound. If the electricity can't go through, it doesn't make any sound.

Electricians use similar devices to check parts of things they're trying to fix. Sometimes a wire may be cut or broken, but is inside or covered up where it can't easily be reached.

Using a circuit like yours, an electrician could touch the ends of the questionable wire to the conductance checker. If the circuit makes noise, the wire is fine. If the circuit is quiet, get out the tools.

This circuit allows you to test whether or not certain objects conduct electricity. After you hook up all the wires, just touch the ends of the two yellow wires to whatever you want to test and listen for a tone. If you hear a beep, you know it's a conductor. Here's how to build your conductance checker:

YELLOW WIRE-20, YELLOW WIRE-4-26, 19-33-36, 27-37-39, 3-35-38, 28-34

Any time someone fixes anything electrical—toy robots, microwave ovens, cars, airliners, space shuttles, battery-powered socks—sooner or later they are going to check some part of it with a conductivity circuit.

You can use the circuit to test things in your house to see if they are conductors or nonconductors. Try the obvious items first, like spoons and Popsicle sticks. Then try some fun stuff. Is a banana a conductor? How about a slice of bread?

WARNING!

Do NOT check electrical outlets, light sockets, or anything that is plugged into the wall! The amount of electricity in these things is very, very dangerous.

STRENGTH CHECKER

WHAT'S GOING ON?

You are part of the circuit in this experiment. By holding the foil balls in your hands, you complete the circuit. This time, though, the electricity is going all the way from one hand, across your body, and out the other hand. (Did you glow in the dark? Just kidding.) Squeezing the balls increases how much skin touches the aluminum, allowing more current to reach the oscillator and piezo transducer and making a higher tone. So the harder you squeeze, the higher the tone. That means the person that makes the highest tone is the strongest, right?

Well, almost right. Other things affect how this works, too. If you dampen your hands you will conduct more electricity. Your emotions can also change how much electricity can go through your skin. Sweaty hands and flushed skin also change how well your skin will conduct.

To make this circuit work, you'll need to make two balls of aluminum foil, each big enough to fit into the palm of your hand. After you build the circuit, stick the loose end of each of the yellow wires into one of the aluminum-foil balls so that each ball has a wire in it. It's important that the bare metal ends of the wires touch the aluminum foil. After you connect the battery, hold one ball in each hand. You should hear a buzzing sound. The harder you squeeze them, the higher the tone you will hear. Squeeze as hard as you can to make the tone as high as you can. Here are the connections:

3-35-38, 33-36-YELLOW WIRE, 4-20-21-23, 22-25-34, 24-37-39, 19-YELLOW WIRE

Lie detectors use this type of measurement. A lie detector measures a number of things, such as heartbeat, breathing rate, and how well the skin conducts electricity. The idea is that if you're nervous, you'll start to sweat. Sweat conducts electricity really well. You will also get flushed. This tells the lie detector which questions make you particularly nervous, such as "Who ate my cookies?"

Try this with some of your friends. See who can make the highest tone.

33

ELECTRONIC ROOSTER

WHAT'S GOING ON?

This circuit turns on a buzzer (actually the piezo transducer) when light shines on it. After you connect the battery, you will hear the piezo transducer. Now cover the photocell with your hand. The piezo transducer should turn off. If it's still making noise, try taking the circuit into a dark room; if it turns off, you know the circuit is working properly. Here are the connections:

**6-20-21-23, 19-28-36-38,
5-35, 24-37-39,
18-22-25-34, 1-27-33,
2-17-26**

The most important part of this circuit is the photocell. The more light there is available, the more electricity is produced. This circuit is called the Electronic Rooster because you can put it in your bedroom window at night, and when the sun comes up it will beep at you. And beep and beep and beep until you turn it off.

There are other fun things that you can do with your Electronic Rooster. For instance, if there is anyone in your house who is making late-night refrigerator raids, putting the circuit in the fridge could be entertaining. You could put it in the drawer that your little brother keeps getting into. You could put it on your windowsill to make sure you wake up in time to take the dog for a walk.

ELECTRONIC TAG

"Tag!"
"You're it!"

"Did too!"

"Did too!"

"You didn't touch me! You missed me by a mile!"

"Did not!"

"Did not!"

You'll need at least two people to test this circuit. After you make all the connections, hold one of the yellow wires in your hand. Then have a friend hold the other wire in one of their hands. Now touch each other, making sure you touch skin-to-skin. You should hear the buzzer the instant you touch! Here's how to build electronic tag:

3-35-38, 33-36-YELLOW WIRE, 19-YELLOW WIRE, 4-20-21-23, 24-37-39, 22-25-34

Does this argument sound familiar? Probably everyone in the world has been involved in this fight.

WHAT'S GOING ON?

You have now built an Electronic Tag Detector, a device specially designed to answer this age-old problem! The catch is that each person needs to hold on to a wire connected to your workbench, so running around will probably be a little bit difficult. But it's still cool!

Find a partner and experiment with how sensitive the circuit is. Does a little fingertip touch set it off? Does it work if your partner just touches your sleeve?

Here's a two-person game you can try. Have each person hold one wire, and stand facing each other. One person holds his hand palm up, and the other person holds his hand palm down over the top of it without touching. The person whose hand is below tries to touch the top of the partner's hand before he can pull it away.

You may have played this game before, but now you have an electronic judge!

Actually, the circuit is so sensitive that it will work through as many as six people! Form two chains of three people holding hands. Have one person from each group hold on to a wire. When the people at the other end of the chains touch, the piezo transducer should go off.

35

MORSE CODE GENERATOR

•-- •••• •- - ••• --• --- •• -• --• --- -•

(WHAT'S GOING ON?)

When you touch the wire to the spring, you complete the circuit and send electricity to the piezo transducer.

You now have a telegraph. The first telegraph in the United States was invented in 1837 by Samuel Morse, who also invented the code that was used to send information back and forth over the telegraph. Not surprisingly, this code was and is called Morse code. Morse code is still used today by shortwave radio operators to communicate all across the world.

If you practice a little, you can use Morse code to send messages, too. Letters are spelled out by using "dots" (short sounds) and "dashes" (longer sounds). Try this practice word:

• -••- -•-• • •-•- •-•- • -•- -

By replacing the speaker wire with longer pieces of wire from the hardware store, you can send messages from one room to another.

Here is the basic code:

A	B	C	D	E	F	G	H	I	J	K	L	M
•-	-•••	-•-•	-••	•	••-•	--•	••••	••	•---	-•-	•-••	--

N	O	P	Q	R	S	T	U	V	W	X	Y	Z
-•	---	•--•	--•-	•-•	•••	-	••-	•••-	•--	-••-	-•--	--••

METRONOME

WHAT'S GOING ON?
TICKTOCK, TICKTOCK, TICKTOCK...

You've probably heard an old clock making that noise. The clock's sound comes from a pendulum that swings back and forth at exactly the same speed.

The project you have built doesn't have a pendulum, but the capacitor in it works on a similar principle. It fills up with electricity in exactly the same amount of time, every time. When the capacitor is full, the circuit lets the electricity out, and the piezo transducer beeps. Since the amount of time it takes to fill the capacitor is always the same, it beeps at a nice, even rhythm.

You can use your circuit for a metronome, which is what musicians use to help them practice their music at the right speed (called *tempo* in the music world). You can adjust the beat of the beep by changing the resistor or the capacitor. The resistor controls how fast the electricity is going into the capacitor. If the electricity comes in slowly, the capacitor will take longer to fill up and will make a slow, steady beep. If the electricity comes in quickly, the capacitor will fill up faster and will make a rapid beep.

This circuit makes a "ticktock" sound that's perfect for keeping time to music.
For a faster rhythm, change the following connections: Move the wire from spring 19 to spring 17, and move the wire from spring 20 to spring 15, and add a wire from spring 16 to spring 18. You should now hear a faster "ticktock" sound. Hear are the connections for a slow rhythm:

9-35-38, 19-36-33, 20-10-26, 28-34, 27-37-39

Changing to a large capacitor will also slow down the beat. Switching to a smaller capacitor will produce a faster beat. If you change the resistor and the capacitor, you should be able to make it go really fast or r-e-a-l-l-y s-l-o-w...

For fun, adjust the metronome for a really slow, long beat. Then hide it in the back of your brother's or sister's sock drawer and see if they can find it before it drives them crazy.

EXPERIMENT 19
FLIP-FLOP CIRCUIT
WHAT'S GOING ON?

So what's a flip-flop? It is nothing less than the very heart and soul of computerdom. Deep in the very core of every computer, everything is based on this simple circuit.

A flip-flop is simply a circuit that is changed from on to off and off to on with the same signal. It's like having a special light switch that works with a single button. One button does all the switching, which makes it easy to "flip" the light on and "flop" it back off again.

This circuit remembers which LED is lit. When you touch the wire to a certain spring, the circuit turns off one LED and turns on the other. Once the circuit is built, connect the battery, and the green LED will light up. Now touch the loose lead wire to spring 26, and the red LED will light up and the green LED will go off. Touch the lead wire to spring 23 and the green LED will light up again.
Here's how to build your flip-flop:

11-13-33, 14-32, 15-27-31, 17-26, 18-24-29, 16-23, 25-28-34-YELLOW WIRE, 12-30

Why is this important? Because all computer information is stored as *bits*. A bit is either a "one" or a "zero." These little bits are recorded in little tiny flip-flop circuits where a flip-flop in the ON position means "one," and a flip-flop in the OFF position means "zero." (A flip-flop in any other position means "broken.")

Computers need a ton of flip-flops. (Actually, the circuits in the first computers weighed several tons.) Information is translated into a code—almost like Morse code—that combines groups of ones and zeros to represent letters and numbers. To store one letter of information—let's say a "q"—requires eight bits of information, shown as a pattern that looks something like 10011101. Each one or zero needs a flip-flop. The last paragraph would take over 2,000 flip-flops!

PERSISTENCE-OF-VISION TESTER

This circuit will make an LED blink very quickly. When it blinks fast enough, it will look like it's not blinking at all! After you connect the battery, touch the loose wire to spring 20. The LED will flash slowly. Now touch spring 18, and the LED will flash faster. Next try spring 16. The LED will look like it's not blinking anymore, but it really is. Take your workbench into a dark room and connect the loose wire to spring 16. Gently wave the workbench back and forth and you will see dashes of light. This proves the light is really blinking. Here are the connections:

7-35, 15-17-19-33-36, 8-23-YELLOW WIRE, 25-34, 30-37, 24-29

WHAT'S GOING ON?

This project wants to fool you. You can adjust how quickly the LED flashes, but if you adjust it too far it stops flashing and just stays on. Or does it?

Actually, the light is still flashing—you just can't see it. The reason you don't see the light flashing is because of something called *persistence of vision*, which means that your eyes continue to see a light or a picture for a brief fraction of a second after it's gone. But the light isn't really there! Your eyes are fooled, tricked, bamboozled.

This kind of trickery is used on you every day. Do you ever watch television? You are actually watching one tiny dot of light flashing across the screen at a very high speed. When you go to the movies, you are seeing lots of still pictures being projected at 24 frames per second. We think we see "moving pictures" because our persistence of vision fills in the spaces between the individual pictures.

CONGRATULATIONS

You did it!
(That was a lot of work, too, so you should be pretty impressed with yourself.) But don't put the kit away just yet, because you're actually not done yet.

Why not? Because as much fun as it was to build the projects, it's even better to invent your own! You can take what you've learned from the experiments and try creating your own circuits. If you want, make small changes in some of the circuits so they work a little differently. If you feel really confident in how much you understand the circuits, make bigger changes or start your own from scratch!

Please remember all the safety rules, though—don't get creative with those! Don't use any source of electricity other than the 9-volt battery. And follow all the rules about the delicate components such as transistors—there are lots of easy ways to fry them.